Cats and Kittens

written by Anita Ganeri

illustrated by Anni Axworthy

A⁺
Smart Apple Media

This book has been published in cooperation with Evans Publishing Group.

Copyright © Evans Brothers Limited 2007
Text Copyright © Anita Ganeri 2007
Illustrations Copyright © Anni Axworthy
This edition published under license from Evans Brothers Limited
All right reserved

Published in the United States by Smart Apple Media
2140 Howard Drive West, North Mankato, Minnesota 56003

U.S. publication copyright © 2008 Smart Apple Media
International copyright reserved in all countries.
No part of this book may be reproduced in any form
without written permission from the publisher.
Printed in China

Library of Congress Cataloging-in-Publication Data

Ganeri, Anita, 1961-
Cats and kittens / by Anita Ganeri.
p.cm. - (Animals and their babies)
Includes index.
ISBN 978-1-58340-807-0
1. Kittens—Juvenile literature. 2. Cats—Juvenile literature. I Title.

SF445.7.G365 2007
636.8'07—dc22   2006103527

9 8 7 6 5 4 3 2 1

CONTENTS

A baby cat is called a kitten. When kittens are born, they are small and helpless. They cannot see or hear. They snuggle up to their mother. They wiggle around on their tummies.

Kittens spend a lot of time sleeping and drinking their mother's milk. This is called suckling. The milk helps them to grow bigger and stronger.

A kitten grows quickly. It opens its eyes when it is two weeks old. At first, its eyes are blue and cloudy. It cannot see very well. It also starts to hear.

About a week later, the kitten takes its first, wobbly steps. Now it is ready to leave its mother and go exploring on its own. If the kitten gets frightened, it meows for its mother.

The kittens are bigger and stronger now.
They like to pretend to fight
each other.

This teaches them how to
hunt for food when they are older.

The kittens like to jump and leap. They roll
around on the ground. If they play too roughly,
their mother taps them with her paw.

When the kittens are about six weeks old, they start eating solid food. They eat small meals of kitten food, three to four times a day. They need fresh, clean water to drink.

At first, the mother licks the kittens to keep them clean.

Soon the kittens can wash themselves. They are able to twist around to lick the fur on their backs.

The kittens are eight weeks old now. They are old enough to leave their mother and to be chosen as pets. Caring for a kitten is fun, but it also takes a lot of time. You need to look after it every day.

When your kitten is about 10 weeks old, you must take it to the veterinarian, or vet. The vet gives it an injection to keep it from getting sick.

Kittens have to be trained to use a litter box. Lift your kitten gently into its litter box. Do this often until it learns to use the box on its own.

Kittens have to scratch their claws to keep them sharp. Outside, they can scratch trees. Indoors, a scratching post is best.

17

By the time it is about 12 weeks old, the kitten is not a kitten anymore. It is a young cat! Its coat is thick and glossy. Its eyes are green, blue, yellow, or orange.

The young cat likes to play in the yard. It races around, chasing leaves blown by the wind. It stalks the leaves, then pounces. It loves to climb trees.

The cat is one year old. It is grown up. Male cats grow bigger than female cats. Cats can live for a long time, usually for about 12 to 16 years.

The cat is old enough to have kittens of its own. A male and female cat meet. A few weeks later, the female has kittens. And the kittens will grow into . . . new cats!

Index

Further Information

If you are thinking of getting a kitten as a pet, find out as much as you can about how to care for it. You can find lots of information at www.aspca.org, the official Web site of the American Society for the Prevention of Cruelty to Animals.